Arbor Day

Rebecca Rissman

Heinemann Library
Chicago, Illinois

www.heinemannraintree.com
Visit our website to find out more information about Heinemann-Raintree books.

To order:

☎ Phone 888-454-2279

🖥 Visit www.heinemannraintree.com to browse our catalog and order online.

Edited by Adrian Vigliano and Rebecca Rissman
Designed by Ryan Frieson
Picture research by Tracy Cummins
Leveling by Nancy E. Harris
Originated by Capstone Global Library Ltd.
Printed in China by South China Printing Company Ltd.

15 14 13 12 11 10
10 9 8 7 6 5 4 3 2 1

Library of Congress Cataloging-in-Publication Data
Rissman, Rebecca.
 Arbor Day / Rebecca Rissman.
     p. cm.—(Holidays and festivals)
 Includes bibliographical references and index.
 ISBN 978-1-4329-4064-5 (hc)—ISBN 978-1-4329-4083-6 (pb) 1.
Arbor Day—United States—Juvenile literature. I. Title.
 SD363.R57 2011
 394.262—dc22   2009052908

Acknowledgments

The author and publishers are grateful to the following for permission to reproduce copyright material: Arbor Day Foundation **pp.6**, **10**; Corbis ©Artiga Photo **p.5**; Corbis **pp.12**, **13**; Corbis ©Yi Lu **p.17**; Corbis ©Scott Stulberg **p.20**; Getty Images/Sean Justice **p.4**; Getty Images/Martin Barraud **p.16**; istockphoto ©linearcurves **p.22**; Library of Congress Prints and Photographs Division **pp.7**, **11**, **23**; Shutterstock ©Marilyn Barbone **p. 8**; Shutterstock ©Losevsky Pavel **p.14**; Shutterstock ©Beata Becla **p.15**; Shutterstock ©Eky Chan **p.18**; Shutterstock ©Kzenon **p.19**; Shutterstock ©Ralph Loesche **p.21**; The Granger Collection, New York **p.9**.

Cover photograph of new life tree reproduced with permission of istockphoto ©Wojtek Kryczka. Back cover photograph reproduced with permission of Shutterstock ©Ralph Loesche.

Every effort has been made to contact copyright holders of any material reproduced in this book. Any omissions will be rectified in subsequent printings if notice is given to the publisher.

Contents

What Is a Holiday?

People celebrate holidays.
A holiday is a special day.

Arbor Day is a holiday.

The Story of Arbor Day

J. Sterling Morton was a pioneer in Nebraska. Pioneers were people who looked for new places to live.

There were few trees in Nebraska.
This made life hard for the pioneers.

Trees hold the soil in place. Trees give people and other animals shade.

The pioneers needed wood from trees to build. They needed wood from trees for fire.

Morton told people it was important to plant trees.

He wanted a special day for people
to plant trees.

The first Arbor Day was in 1872.

People planted almost one million trees that day!

Trees Are Important

Trees are even more important than Morton thought.

Now we know that trees help keep the air clean.

Celebrating Arbor Day

On Arbor Day people plant trees.

People spend time outdoors.
People pick up litter.

People remember how trees help the Earth.

People remember how trees help us.

Arbor Day Symbols

Trees are symbols of Arbor Day.

Arbor comes from the word for tree in Latin.

Arbor Day Near You

Arbor Day is celebrated at different times of the year. Find out when Arbor Day is in your state.

Picture Glossary

 **pioneer** people who move to new places to live. J. Sterling Morton was a pioneer.

Index

Note to Parents and Teachers

Before reading

Talk about the importance of trees. Ask the children to think about the ways trees contribute to our Earth – how they keep us cool, clean the air, and provide homes for animals and birds. Ask the children to share some experiences they've had with trees. What would it be like without trees? Explain that there is a special holiday just for celebrating trees.

After reading

Organize a tree-planting event. Invite a diverse range of community members to help plant the trees. Ask everyone to share a poem, song or story that celebrates trees.